Spiritual Retreats

A Guide to Slowing Down to be with God

Jean Wise

Spiritual Retreats: A Guide to Slowing Down to be with God
Copyright © 2016 by Jean Wise

ISBN -13: 978-0-9668688-3-9

Learn more information at: www.healthyspirituality.org

Dedication

Never would I have discovered all the treasures waiting
for me in the practice of going on a retreat if it were not
for my friend and mentor, Nancy Brousseau.
Her guidance, direction, and "push to dive deeper"
motivated me to attend that first time of slowing down
to be with God and I have never regretted going.
Nancy shared so many resources and wisdom over the
years – I will be forever grateful. Thank you, Nancy.
This book is dedicated to you in the hope it will bless
many more people in their walk with God.

Introduction

I start getting anxious about the middle of Georgia. I stare out the window to capture the first glimpse. My foot taps impatiently and I rock back and forth thinking my motion will propel the car faster.

Finally, I see one.

A palm tree! My husband jumps as I squeal. I see one, I tell him. Palm trees slowly begin to appear as we near Florida.

My patient husband has long endured my excitement when we travel south. Leaving dreary Ohio in the middle of February for a few weeks of Florida sunshine and warmth energizes my soul. I spend weeks anticipating, planning, envisioning our time there.

We celebrate the arrival at the state line by stopping at the Florida Welcome Center conveniently located on the border right off Interstate 75.

Friendly smiles welcome us. Orange juice – the official nectar of Florida - refreshes our spirit.

Stretching stiff muscles, we stroll around the grounds, reading the local history and deeply breathing in the warmer air. I seek out informational maps to guide us further and to explore new destinations. Tour directors willingly answer our questions to help us with our discoveries.

We rest. We smile. We continue on our way south with our hands, hearts, and minds jam-packed with info, inspiration, and ideas.

Not much different from how I feel about going on a spiritual retreat. Of course withdrawing from the world to spend time with God is far from my Florida touristy, self-promoting oasis. But the preparation for the trip, the experience I gather while there, and the memories and lessons I take home are similar.

A spiritual retreat is an opportunity to slow down to spend time with God. Leaving behind the routine of everyday life, retreats can be a vacation with God. We explore, we learn new things, we experience the world differently. We see ourselves in a new light. We talk and listen deeply. We leave refreshed and ready to reenter the world.

The pleasure and rewards of taking a vacation start with the anticipation of the event, embracing the present while on the trip, then reliving and enjoying the memories once home. These three sections also drive the delight and lessons experienced while on a spiritual retreat.

Spiritual Retreats, A Guide to Slowing Down to be with God is a manual for you to explore this practice. The first section offers ideas on how to prepare ahead, what to anticipate and the benefits and logistics of attending a retreat setting.

The second part of this book gives practices to explore while on a retreat, plus what to carry with you, both physically and in your mind and heart.

The third section invites us to pause before the re-entry into the noisy post retreat world. How do we come down from a mountaintop experience and bring with us all the lessons and insights we learn to apply to the daily living? How can we continue to slow down with God in the chaos of everyday life?

It is my hope these words bless your practice, encourage you to take retreats and make the most of this sacred time with God. Get out a journal or pen and paper to take notes on what you want to try. Be honest in identifying the excuses that prevent you from going on a retreat and letting go of past experiences. And pray. Ask God if the practice of a spiritual retreat is for you in this season of your life.

BLESSING

Slow down – it's time to pause.

Come away with the Lord and get some rest.

Breathe in deeply.

Let go of the world's noise and your ego's chattering.

Imagine God taking you by the hand and inviting you to linger awhile with him.

Shhh – listen to the voice of your own heart and the loving nearness of God's heartbeat.

Hear your dreams, concerns, and desires within God's reassuring guidance.

Remember you are God's beloved child and he waits for you.

May this time of slowing down to be with God deepen your faith, light your way, and draw you closer to Him.

Pause to Prepare: Preplanning Before the Retreat

Come with me by yourselves to a quiet place
and get some rest.
Mark 6: 31

Are you a planner or do you live more spontaneously? Some of us love the organization, the research, and sense of control knowing everything ahead of time. We know what to expect and when it will happen. The anticipation is part of the satisfaction of the journey.

Other people love the adventure of discovery when they arrive at their destination and prefer not to have the hindrance of a schedule or constraints of a plan. Their impulsive personalities thrive on winging it through unstructured life experiences.

Neither approach to life is wrong and the degree of preplanning wanted and needed before going on retreat varies with each individual.

How you approach slowing down with God on a retreat is similar. Preplanning can be adapted to your preference. Most people do need a little basic preparation before a retreat, so the basic questions are answered, necessary items are packed, and you arrive less stressed for your time with God.

If you haven't been on a retreat before, you may have never really considered what a retreat was and what benefits might be gained by attending one. You may have no idea what happens while you are there. There are different types of retreats – which one best suits you for where you are now in your faith?

Fear may attack you as you wonder if this may draw you into a cult or you will feel so uncomfortable you want to escape. Even the idea of *"can you escape once you are there"* may have entered your mind.

The main antidote for fear is prayer followed by facts. Ask God for the wisdom to know what you need to make a clear decision on when and what type of retreat is best for you. Then, even with some anxieties still churning in your tummy, put the fears aside.

Let's explore the basics about going on a retreat.

The Basics – What is a retreat?

A retreat is simply a time away with God. A break from routine. Getting out of your normal rut and finding a quiet interlude and place to slow down with God. You create space in your calendar, your surroundings, and in your heart for God.

Jesus frequently took the time for prayer with his father. Jesus models for us this powerful spiritual discipline.

> **One of those days Jesus went out to a mountainside to pray and spent the night praying to God.**
> **Luke 6: 12**

Some people describe a retreat as a vacation with God and as a time to relax in his presence. Sometimes our biggest need and want is just to rest. The tensions of life tangle our nerves and we long to unwind.

We may be dry and need nourishment. We feel off-centered and want to recalibrate. We can't hear God in the midst of the noisy reality and hunger for more of him.

Maybe a question is stirring within us, a restlessness gnawing for an answer. Discernment may be our primary motivator and a retreat the opportunity to sort and sift options.

God created us to be in a healthy relationship with him. Perhaps we are missing our time with him and a retreat is a time to deepen our friendship with God.

Retreats are a refreshing oasis for our soul. A sanctuary for worship, focus, and rest.

A retreat is simply a matter of going into a separate place to seek Christian growth in a disciplined way. Retreat offers us the grace to be ourselves in God's presence without self-consciousness, without masquerade. Retreat proves the chance to be both physically and spiritually refreshed.
Emilie Griffin

Our spirits may be tired. Our souls empty. We get caught in the shallow busyness of life instead of the deeper peace we know is there.

Every so often I need out; something will throw me into total disproportion, and I have to get away from everybody – away from all those people I love most in the world – in order to regain a sense of proportion.
Madeleine L'Engle.

Do introverts crave retreats more than extroverts?
Introverts draw their renewing energy from silence and

stillness. They crave time alone, away from people, noise, and craziness of conflicting demands.

As an introvert, I can tell when I haven't been on a retreat for a while. I feel more restless, less focused. I yearn to reconnect with God on a deeper level that I can't find in the routines of everyday life. I sense an invitation to draw nearer to him in silence. It is time to attend to my soul. I now intentionally plan to attend a silent retreat at least on a yearly basis as part of my regular spiritual practice.

Extroverts grow more with interactions with others. Take heart, Extroverts – retreats can also be for you.

Preached retreats where there is more talking and connecting with others may be a good starting place. But even silent retreats fulfill a need within the extrovert. A sense of community emerges among retreatants experiencing the same environment, eating meals in silent, and walking together with God. The body of Christ communicates with each other without words and noise in amazing ways.

All personality types can learn from various kinds of retreats. Withdrawing for a time of gathering thoughts together, hearing God in new ways, and flourishing in a safe and restful space far from the craziness of the world is a practice not quite like any other.

Very early in the morning, while it was still dark, Jesus got up, left the house and went off to a solitary place, where he prayed.
Mark 1: 35

Where will you go for a retreat?

You could simply retreat with God in your living room. Or at a local hotel. Or a cabin by a lake. Maybe the family will be gone on their own weekend adventure and you use this opportunity for quiet time with God.

This type of retreat of designing your own retreat at home may be the only option for some people due to commitment, finances, and life demands. Even striving to focus on God for one hour each week enriches our faith.

I find staying at home too distracting and, to be honest, I am tempted by the routines, the to-do list, and the *"maybe I can get just one load of wash done."* Getting away to new places helps to break the normal habits and leads to more focused time with God with less interruptions.

Retreat Logistics

Many areas now have retreat centers within driving distance. I have included some resources in the back of this book to help you locate a retreat center.

Call a local church to ask about nearby locations of a retreat center. Ask a minister, priest, or spiritual director. Ask someone you know who has talked about going on retreats.

Home or away, at a retreat center or a friend's cottage in the woods, you can find a place of peace, quiet, and space for God.

Length

The length of the retreat can vary widely. If you are anxious you may want to try a half-day at first. Overnight is always a little better as I have found it takes me quite a while to unwind from the world and settle into a retreat routine.

Weekend retreats are very common, starting on Friday night and finishing Sunday afternoon. Some retreat centers also offer Monday through Friday time frames.

If you find a retreat you are interested in, but the time or length just doesn't fit for some reason, call the center director and discuss if there are other options. I have been on retreats where someone arrives a bit late or leaves early. Of course you miss the full effect, but still those people gained some benefits from their time away.

I find a three night/four-day length works well for me. This length provides enough time for me to settle in, to let go, to enjoy a walk on the grounds, to be with God. The time is long enough to experience God deeply, yet I can get back to my home, my work and my routine in a timely manner.

Even longer retreats are available, such as two weeks or 30 days. The month-long retreat is often called a 30-day Ignatius Retreat based on St. Ignatius Spiritual Exercises. This longer retreat includes times of daily prayer, reflection, and spiritual direction.

Types of Retreats

Just as there are a variety of options for length of retreats, you have many choices in types of retreats.

Preached Retreats. A speaker or several speakers present a topic on a specific theme.

The schedule for a preached retreat vary considerably. Sometimes the days are full with back to back presentations, but often these types of retreats also provide time for small group discussion and even quiet reflection. This is a great place to start for someone who has never attended a retreat. Time is set aside to explore the center's grounds and also time for shared worship, or special times of prayer, art, or creativity.

You can get on a retreat center's mailing list to find out about upcoming retreats. The theme or the speaker or perhaps an author you have read may pique your interest.

Individual Retreats –You can set up a retreat on your own or with a small group. Often these are silent retreats where you may or may not meet daily for about an hour with a spiritual director. You create your own schedule (more on that in the next chapter) and simply rest, read, and reflect.

You might also consider a "quiet day." Many retreat centers are open for individuals to come for just a day. You could pick a certain theme for yourself, such as reading on a topic you are interested in or being creative with art or music for the day.

Why Go on a retreat?

The primary reason to go on a retreat is to *"let your soul catch up with your body."*

What better reason to attend a retreat than to rest, recalibrate and become whole again in the presence of God?

The expression *"let your soul catch up with your body"* comes from a story that has circulated for a long time: In the Himalayan mountains, Sherpas guide the climbers and carry the equipment up the rugged paths. There is a story that Sherpas have been known to stop suddenly after a time of leading, encouraging, and escorting the company.

Without much explanation, they put down their burdens and rest as if they were waiting for something or someone.

Westerners get impatient with this *"waste of time"* and want to keep pushing forward. The *"get it done attitude"* is so dominant in our culture. Beat the clock. Accomplish this task.

When asked why they stop, the Sherpas answer, *"We are waiting for our souls to catch up with our bodies."*

Our minds race ahead and we drive our bodies into fatigue. Our emotional bank is empty, but we think we can accomplish just a few more things.

Our souls walk at a different pace, often slower, more intentional, and to a Godly beat. No wonder we feel scattered, shattered, and disconnected in our culture. Time to find some time to allow our souls to catch up and bring us whole again.

Times of extended retreat give us a chance to come home to ourselves in God's presence and to bring the realities of our life to God in utter privacy. This is important for us and for those we serve.... On retreat we rest in God and wait on him to do what is needed. Eventually we return to the battle with fresh energy and keener insight.
Ruth Haley Baron

Retreats create the space to be with God. To hear him in new and deeper ways. To discern a next step.

We often see a new perspective of our lives, an experience, a memory when we enter into a change of place, of routine and a reduction of noise levels.

The best retreats for me are a blend of nutrition for my heart and mind. I love the combination of time to read and listen mixed with rest, reflection, and journaling.

I come away with an improved sense of God at the center of my life. I leave feeling balanced and energized.

Remember the old dials we had on the radio? Sometimes we had to move them just slightly to hear the voice clearer and without interference. A retreats reset our internal dial to hear God better.

To be honest, the only reason I experienced my very silent retreat was because it was a class requirement for my spiritual direction course. But I continue because the time of slowing down with God nourishes me like no other practice.

You will discover your own reasons to attend a retreat and they may evolve over time. Be open. Pray. Listen.

What's Stopping You?

We are people who love excuses. We create our own excuses at times and may not even realize it. To be honest it isn't easy to go on a retreat.

We don't have the time. How will the family manage? Work won't exist without me. The world will crash if I go. Will other people judge me as *"holier than thou"*?

You may have mixed feelings about going. You know you need the time away, but the anxiety of what will happen distracts us and churns within us. Often we may worry about *"what if nothing happens."*

Maybe we live in quiet all day long and the thought of more silence is deafening or too frightening for us. We may even just be too tired to think about getting away.

Yes, it feels safer to stay in our comfort zones, but how will we refresh our spiritual life and hear God more deeply if nothing changes? Remember how Albert Einstein defined insanity:

Doing the same thing over and over again and expecting different results.

Listen to yourself and honestly identify what excuses you are telling repeatedly. Are they real? What are your options?

What to expect on retreat

Often the brochure and website will give you a peek into what will happen on the retreat you plan to attend. A tentative agenda, ideas of what to bring, maybe an article or book will be mentioned.

The retreat center website is another source of information.

Here are some questions to consider in preparation for the retreat:

- What are the sleeping rooms like?
- What essentials do I need to bring?
- I have learned to ask if the rooms have fans or air conditioning.
- Can I get an extra pillow?
- Is there an alarm clock?
- Are there shared or private bathrooms?

- Ask about meals –what are the meal times and cost and is there a place to store/share snacks and refreshments?
- Do you have any special needs to consider such as mobility or diet restrictions?
- Can you walk the grounds and use the rooms throughout the facility?
- If it is a silent retreat, how does that work? For example, are meals eaten in silence?
- What are the costs? Are there any scholarships or work programs available to offset the cost?
- Is there a schedule available?
- Are there set worship/prayer times that you might participate in?
- Is there a spiritual director available for appointments and is this an additional cost?

Don't get bogged down with these details though. The most important item to have ready and bring with you is this:

An open and willing heart – receptive to God.

Places to go

Inner and outer spaces create an environment to explore all these benefits of a retreat.

External Space. Ask around and research retreat centers. Look for an environment that appeals to your spirit. What is the setting? Will it be distracting?

Though not necessary, I check for a place with walking trails and outdoors. The older centers with rich paneling and small nooks and crannies to explore pique my interest. And I adore ones with a library, full of interesting resources.

Internal Space. Spend a few minutes before a retreat in preparing the inner space of your heart. What is your intention/deep desire for this time away? Is there a word or Bible verse calling you? A theme?

As I was getting ready to write this book, I posted on my blog about my upcoming retreat and how I was preparing for this time away. Can you tell I am a planner? I love to know the details and what to expect. I freely admit this feeds my sense of control.

I have learned though, to look, explore, then let go and enjoy the time away, worry-free.

Don't waste your life in doubts and fears: spend yourself on the work before you, well assured that the right performance of this hour's duties will be the best preparation for the hours or ages that follow it.
Ralph Waldo Emerson

A good friend read that blog post about preparing for retreat at the time when she too was getting ready to leave for her first silent retreat. She leans much more to spontaneity and no constraints and my words produced some panic within her heart. She said to me, *"Oh no! I have to do all this thinking ahead of time? There is no time. I don't want to do this."*

And she is right too. She did not have to deliberate all these details and speculate all the possibilities.

Prepare as you need to. As you want to. God will be there waiting for you no matter how you come, when you arrive or what you bring with you. Trust him. He wants to spend this time with you and can't wait to be with you.

Come with an open and willing heart. Empty your head and your hands. Arrive ready to talk and listen and be with God. That is all you really need to pack.

Imagine yourself as a living house. God comes in to rebuild that house. At first, perhaps, you can understand what He is doing. He is getting the drains right and stopping the leaks in the roof and so on; you knew that those jobs needed doing and so you are not surprised. But presently He starts knocking the house about in a way that hurts abominably and does not seem to make any sense. What on earth is He up to?
The explanation is that He is building quite a different house from the one you thought of - throwing out a new wing here, putting on an extra floor there, running up towers, making courtyards. You thought you were being made into a decent little cottage: but He is building a palace. He intends to come and live in it Himself.
C.S. Lewis

Questions to Ponder:

1. Are you spontaneous or a detailed planner or some degree in-between?

2. If you attended a retreat before, what do you wish you had known ahead of time?

3. What questions do you need to ask someone before attending a retreat?

Blessing

Come!

Come with an open and willing heart.

Come to be with God and hear him in new ways.

Come to rest.

Slow down and be present in the present for the Presence.

Welcome the tears, the silence, the letting go of burdens.

Say hello to yourself hidden deep under the clutter of daily distractions, noise, and challenges of everyday life.

May you find what you are seeking and longing for.

May you be still and commune with God.

Pause to be Present: The Actual Retreat Experience

But Jesus often withdrew to lonely places and prayed.
Luke 5:16

Why did I ever sign up for this thing?

I was just too busy to go. The to-do list demanded my presence. The urgent ruled my time with loud commands. How could I stop with so many balls to juggle in the air of my life?

My heart ached and longed for some time away, but my head, in its cerebral best logic with its undergirding of fear arising from the primitive brain stem, diverted my attention. The important drowned in the noisy urgent.

What had I done?

How could I leave the family? My work? The insistent mandate for the necessity of cleaning the toilet and polishing the baseboards. I can be quite skilled at procrastination.

The date for the retreat loomed in my mind and growled in my gut. I didn't want to go. What would happen? I know, I could say we had a death in the family. Or maybe I would get sick. Or what if I had car trouble?

The spiritual formation course I was taking required going on a silent retreat at some point. I had no choice. I felt like a condemned convict being dragged to the gallows.

So I packed. I took lots of ammunition – books, snacks, my laptop - in case boredom or the need to escape from feeling uncomfortable attacked my ego. I lugged enough stuff up to my retreat room to last four weeks instead of four days.

I brought along a ton of weighty expectations, worries, and noise with me too.

My *"brave"* intentions faded as I drove up the winding driveway to the retreat center. I sat in the parking lot for a few minutes.

Then I remembered to pray.

The fear behind my hesitation came from not knowing what to expect. In addition, finding the time for a retreat was a challenge and making all the arrangements to leave burdensome.

God reminded me of my priorities: yes, my family is one of my top values, but so is God and my self-care. Spending time with God reinserted its importance in my life. I felt calmer.

What did I decide in my moment of panic about that first retreat?

I opened the car door.
I entered the retreat center.
I survived.

I actually thrived and came home refreshed and with a new attitude towards going on retreats.

What is the actual retreat experience like? What do I need to bring with me? How can I be fully present?

Packing

He who would travel happily must travel light.
-Antoine de Saint-Exupéry

Pack light. I tend to take too much stuff with me whenever I travel, including going on retreat. My hubby lifts the suitcase into the car with a loud grunt and a mumbling about taking the weighted anvil with me. I am working on this personality fault, but have to remember and be intentional to pack light.

If you wish to travel far and fast, travel light. Take off all your envies, jealousies, unforgiveness, selfishness and fears.
Cesare Pavese

The question become not what to bring, but what NOT to bring.

Excess baggage is a symptom of something we are missing on the inside – a fear that we won't be accepted for what we are, as if our selves are not enough. We bring too much of our past experience, the clutter of our emotions. These things get in the way and keep us from getting close to others. Then we are left with the task of having to find someone else to carry it, whether it is our luggage or our loneliness.
-Mary Morris

What do you really need while on retreat? Here are some ideas to help you pack:

The first thing to pack is your open and willing spirit. I leave behind my compulsion to know what will happen every moment and my need to control and plan.
Sometimes I actually write those words on a paper and put

them on my desk, leaving them there to pick up later. The physical action helps convince my mind and heart to let go.

I ask God for a receptive and amendable attitude. Open to wherever he leads and willing to listen, be vulnerable, and follow his voice. This is difficult for those of us who like to be in charge and know exactly what the next step will be. This prayer surrounds and underpins each retreat as I leave behind my expectations and pack only what I truly need.

What do I take?

- Comfortable clothes.

- Walking shoes.

- Sweater or jacket in case the space is chilly.

- If the rooms don't come with one, an alarm clock may be helpful. I know one person tells me he brings a small timer with him to help him focus for longer periods of time.

- Comfort items like snacks, favorite beverages, and an extra pillow.

What about books? I always take my Bible and my journal. Sometimes if a book has been calling to me, I pack it. I know a few people bring along a classic that they have been wanting to read whenever they finally found the time.

For example, the past two years I have been studying, listening to, and walking with the Desert Mothers and Fathers. On my last retreat, I brought along several books about them and a devotional based on their wisdom.

But books can also be seductive and a temptation, luring you away from God instead of drawing you closer to him. I now leave most books at home, which is very difficult for me because my fear whispers, *"what if I would need them. What if I get bored?"* But I love to read, don't I deserve to use this time for something pleasurable too? Books are always an internal battle for me to decide what to take and what to leave at home.

Books can be useful, but often I find myself spending time with other people's voices instead of hearing my own or God's. I create a pile of books to take with me more out of *FOMO – Fear of Missing Out –* and not having something with me instead of trusting God and his transforming process.

Occasionally, I pack my e-reader, just in case I do want to look up a certain book mentioned by the spiritual director or I see referred to in another writing. Having my e-reader handy allows me to download the book immediately. But in all honesty, packing it "just in case" is a crutch and an excuse.

Less is better.

Slowly, I am learning to leave the books behind and trust God to provide. And he does.

My journal is the one book I always take. Some years I take several – the most current one and one from the past year. I find the first night of the retreat when my mind is still full and I am uncertain how to settle in, rereading my journals and my Bible quiets my spirit. The noise drips off my finger tips and tension sheds like an old snake skin.

Other people love to pack their favorite art material. One year I watched a fellow retreatant sketch pencil drawings of our beautiful outdoor surroundings and weave in her favorite Bible verses into the drawings. The process provided relaxation, a centering practice and a memorable symbol for her to mark this time away and where she was on her spiritual journey.

Bring along a favorite pen. I have several styles that make me feel special when I use them. I love how they fit my hand and how the ink flows easily. Of course, you don't really have to – any pen will do, but having something comfortable and pleasing in my hands enhances the writing.

Along with my pens, I usually pack colorful post-it notes and highlighters to mark special passages.

Of course, you will need your basic hygiene supplies. I always pack shampoo, conditioner, and my hair dryer as most retreat centers are not hotels providing all those incidentals. There usually is a small token of supplies and they readily will help you if you forget something, but plan ahead what you will need.

Prepare your heart for a spiritual retreat

Always surround your retreat in prayer. Ask God to start now even before you leave, to quiet your internal chattering, so you can listen deeply to his voice. Ask for protection for your time away. Ask God to be with your family, so your worries can stay at home and not rattle your spirit while you are gone.

Is there a Bible verse or image that has resonated lately with you that might be a good place to start at the beginning of the retreat? Make a list of potential ideas.

Sometimes I bring a few things from my home altar to create an environment in my room similar to my sacred space at home. Most retreat centers forbid lighted candles in the rooms due to the fire hazard, so I have a battery operated flickering candle ready to take that I will turn on to open each of my prayer sessions.

A retreat starts well before your arrival at the retreat center. God is constantly at work cultivating the soil of your heart for his word. Remember that a third of the fun on a vacation are the weeks before – in the anticipation of the trip – the second third occurs while you are there, and the last third happens at home – enjoying the memories.

A retreat is much of the same, but too often the busyness, noise, and tension of life steals away the joy, lessons, and groundwork in the time before we leave. Prayer calms and directs us in this season before. And what if life just interrupts and we don't prepare? God will show up mightily anyway. He loves spending time with us and eagerly awaits us, no matter how we arrive or how frazzled we come into his presence.

A word of caution: Don't bring your laptop and work. I want to be honest here in admitting I have occasionally packed a file thinking just maybe I would work a bit. When I fall into that compulsion, the world drags me back to its noise and frazzling demands. Learn from my mistake and leave the work at home for the best retreat experience.

Confession: I still bring my cell phone. Just in case of emergency, I tell myself. I have also used it on occasion to look up a book or topic that I am pondering or search for a lyric or hymn. I will admit I do check my emails. What I have learned that works for me is I only read them once a day and keep the phone on silent. No texting and definitely no Angry Bird head bopping.

I love photography and taking pictures can be a form of prayer called "*visio divina*" or divine seeing. I use my cell phone camera or bring along a camera to capture the scenery, special insights, and memories.

On one retreat, I slowly walked their labyrinth. As I looked down, watching my feet take one step at a time, I noticed a small red ant along the brick pavement, lugging a stone twice as big as he was. He moved with ease, with determination, and focused alone on accomplishing the task before him. He had no idea I was watching from above.

I snapped a photo of my tiny friend and the picture remains in my journal as a remembrance and a treasure from the retreat. That experience inspired much conversation with God that day – What burdens am I hauling? How is God watching over me? Even with burdens, how am I called to the task I am given?

Finally, remember simply to pack light. Leave behind the worries and concerns that occupy your heart and mind. This is your time with God. Come and enjoy his presence.

Expectations/Intentions

Though expectations create tight boundaries on the retreat experience, most people slow down to be with God for a specific purpose. What is your purpose for taking this retreat? What is your intention?

Finding the words to express what you are seeking while on retreat is helpful to add clarity and motivation for paying attention. I often put my desires in the form of a written prayer in my journal before I go. Then I give it up to God as a possibility, something I would like, but tell him he is in charge. My head and heart are now open to receive whatever God wants me to have and to hold.

Other intentions to consider may be discerning a next step, seeking affirmation of where you are presently, enjoying time with God in deep conversations with him and just being with God. Your intention can be as general or as specific as you want.

Begin to gather your thoughts about which prayerful activities you may want to engage in: journaling, pondering goals, assessing your life, doing a word study from the Bible, taking a nap (yes, napping can be prayer too), going for walks with God, worshipping, sitting quietly in the chapel, reading the Bible or studying a specific book.

I take the time before leaving to pause and listen to God. Sometime I review what I have recently recorded in my journal and note questions, themes, and repeating desires. Is there a word I have been hearing lately that may be inviting me to ponder deeper in the time away?

Ask yourself this question: what do I hope to receive from the Lord on this retreat?

I try to hear God before the retreat begins – sometime his voice is clear, but often it isn't. I ask myself what it is I am seeking? Lord, how do you want me to pray in our time together? Where do I feel God is inviting me? What do I most need at this time? I actually write this out in my journal. I pray about what I think is his direction. Then I let my urge to control go.

With open hands, I surrender my intention and expectations to God. I hold them lightly with palms upward. My breath prayer is *"open and willing, Lord."*

Rhythms

The type of retreat determines the schedule or rhythms of the day. Quiet times may be preassigned, but many retreats are completely open. I am always surprised even with unscheduled times how quickly a routine develops on a retreat.

Retreats should always leave space to hear God - time to just be with him.

Sometimes how you spend the entire retreat time is up to you and at first that may be a bit overwhelming. What do I do with all this open time? An uncluttered day can be both scary and freeing.

Be flexible and open to change. I find a loose schedule frames the day combined with periods of intense focus and prayer mingled with rest and recreation. A flexible schedule keeps me focused.

If most of the time is open, formatting my day in blocks of time is helpful. Personally, I don't "assign" specific minutes, but think in ranges such as after breakfast, time before lunch, sometime this afternoon, etc.

Decide what time you need to wake up. Is there a prearranged breakfast time slot? Do you want to skip breakfast and give yourself permission to sleep in for a change? Maybe you know you do better getting up at your usual time. I like to get up, get ready, and take a walk before breakfast, for example.

Are there any set times occurring during the retreat? Even on unscheduled silent retreats, you may have a set time each day to meet with a spiritual director. The retreat organizers may provide a special community prayer experience in the evening.

Many facilities invite the retreatants to participate in the daily prayers or "prayers of the day" as often or as little as wanted. They may chant the Psalms and usually visitors have a booklet to follow along with them.

You may want to block off time for prayer, journaling, art work, or napping. Reserve time to do nothing. Don't over plan your day.

On my last retreat I found an intimate third story sun room. The wind roared that day at 30, 40 and sometimes 50 miles per hour. I sat in that room all afternoon, something I hadn't preplanned at all. I had a front row seat as nature presented a wild and wonderful performance just for me.

Mesmerized by the racing clouds playing hide and seek with the sun, I watched God's creation dance. Large black birds floated on the wind currents. The top branches of the trees swirled and swayed. I closed my eyes and listened to the powerful wind. Refreshing cool air seeped through the windows. I marveled at God's power and imagination. I sensed the presence of the Holy Spirit throughout all creation, even within my heart. To this day, the memory of that afternoon spent with God, unexpected, unplanned and unscheduled, fortifies my spirit.

Arrange a time to read a key Bible verse slowly and prayerfully. Examples may be given to you by the retreat center staff. You may have preselected several verses before the retreat. Maybe there is a topic or theme you want to read about in the Bible.

One year I studied the word *wisdom*. Another year I explored the story of Hagar. I planned certain times of the day to spend intentionally in contemplation with the Bible.

There are no rules for a schedule when setting the agenda yourself. Change it as you wish, but remember that blocks of time provide a rhythm and shape for your day.

One last point on the schedule: it may vary from day to day on a retreat.

The first night is a time of letting go. The noise begins to drip from my body. I shake off the worries and the Holy Spirit blows the dust on my soul. I am usually more restless and fidgety the first evening of my arrival. We are surrounded by so much noise in the world we live in that the silence of the center is jarring, awkward, and uncomfortable. Thoughts and doubts attack me. I fear not hearing God and wasting my time.

Later during the retreat, I sink into a pattern that fits for that particular time with God. I relax, adjust, and walk more leisurely. I slow down with God.

How do we begin?

The first steps vary with the type of retreat.

If it is a preached retreat or where someone or a group is presenting, they will have an initial activity planned. An ice breaker or get to know each other activity may be offered. Often there is music and may be an introductory presentation.

Many preached retreats also have time for quiet reflection and small group sharing. Deepening often comes with the sharing and time alone. If you can, go for a walk. Spend time silently with God. Practice walking and eating at a slower pace to match God's timing.

Try new practices. I laughed as I typed those last three words as I resist some activities offered at some retreats. One place wanted us all to create a mandala – or a geometric art form that helps with meditation. I am the world's worse artist. I can't draw. I rolled my eyes at this type of exercise, but I dove in.

The simple drawing I created meant nothing to anyone else, but spoke tons to me as I thought about my relationship with God and where I was in this season of life.

I almost missed this opportunity to be with God thought art if I hadn't been open to trying a new practice. My sloppy doodle lives permanently in my journal as a keepsake and a marker for my spiritual journey.

A silent retreat can be more challenging to get started, especially the first time you experience extended times of quiet and unscheduled periods of silence. You may not know how to begin.

Many silent retreats begin with a meal with all the retreatants before silence is entered. Often a group meeting to answer questions and provide guidance is part of this gathering.

If you are retreating by yourself, you may want to think about how to first commence your time with God.

Lauren Guest suggests in her book, *Wrapped in Stillness*, to start with a symbolic opening ceremony for your retreat.

An opening ceremony is deeply personal and generally utilizes music, rhythm, objects and symbolic gestures. These elements allow you to build a bridge between your inner self and your intention. There are no rules for an opening ceremony and no one can judge what is appropriate for you. Explore technique until you find what works. Your goal is to be totally present in the moment.

I have never done this type of ritual, but find simply unpacking, setting up things I brought from home for atmosphere, and exploring the facilities or taking a long walk are the early steps for me.

On a silent retreat, it is like entering a threshold of quiet. The eyes of my heart need time to adjust to the new lighting. I am amazed at both the absence of noise and the profound almost touchable presence of silence.

The first evening I slow down, read my journal, and just sit, allowing the tension of driving, arranging and planning and noise to drip from my soul. Sometimes I have to go to various places within the retreat center to enter into the silence. I seek a setting that soothes my spirit and invites me inward.

The next day I slowly go deeper and those larger blocks of time become holy interactions with God. It feels like a process of peeling off the layers. Surprises and discoveries emerge. I slow down with God.

Helpful Faith Practices

Spiritual practices are not ways of forcing God to be with us. God is always with us. Certain disciplines slow us down, help us to let go and listen more deeply, and hear God in new ways.

Faith practices that I find are beneficial on retreat are listed here to serve as a resource, not a to-do list. You may find yourself resting more than being in active prayer and journaling. The next retreat you may feel restless and want to try something new.

Be open and willing to try new spiritual practices, rely on the ones you know and love, or just sit quietly being with God. Remember no rules – only God's wonderful possibilities.

Prayer -A whole new book could be written about all the various forms of prayer to try on a retreat. Sometimes I need the comfort of the ones I am familiar with. Other times I want to stretch myself by trying a new approach to talking and listening with God. Use whatever prayer seems most natural to you.

The quieter, slowing types of prayer work for most retreats. These include centering prayer, breath prayers, and the prayer of quiet. Prayers of thankfulness and praise also surface.

The Christian writer Catherine Marshall shared a prayer that has accompanied me on several retreats – the prayer of relinquishment. This is a prayer of letting go, surrendering whatever we are more attached to than God.

Not my will, but yours be done.
Luke 22: 42

This time of self-emptying leads to release and hope. But like a caterpillar emerging from a cocoon, I struggle. The process takes time. As I give myself completely to God, trusting him with all I hold most dear, the closeness and love from God permeates the time we share together.

Writing in a journal – Even if you don't normally keep a journal, recording your prayers, insights, and questions brings clarity and holds the wisdom learned from a retreat. Writing down the words, sometimes searching to find just the right word to describe how you are feeling or what you are experiencing opens you up to see with new eyes.

Write as you are comfortable, not worrying about sentence structure or spelling. Draw if you want to in your journal if that is helpful. Write a letter to God. Write a letter to yourself from God.

Bible reading - Any form of digging deeper into the scriptures benefits our spirit. Sometimes I explore a person or spend time with the Psalms.

Have you tried Lectio Divina or sacred reading? This form of prayerful reading of the scripture follows a rhythm of reading the material four times. Read the passage slowly and reflectively, listening for a word or phrase or image to shimmer or resonate with you. Spend time with God about that feeling.

The second time you read or hear those words, meditate on them, chew on them to get the full flavor, allow them to sink into your soul.

Read the words once more, this time praying, talking, and listening with God about that passage.

Read the scripture one last time allowing yourself simply to rest in the holy word of God.

Devotional Readings – The resources we have available for devotional readings are amazing. Bring along a book with short entries of a Bible reading and reflection. This could be a devotional book you follow at home or a new one just for the retreat.

Slowing down – Intentionally walk and eat slowly while on retreat. You may want to actually rise from your chair at a slower pace. Take more deep breaths. Put your fork down between bites. Take the time to observe details. Close your eyes and listen to the hum of the building.

Reflection questions – What questions are bubbling inside you while on retreat? What questions did you bring to discuss with God? The purpose of questions is to name what is calling you and sort through what you may be hearing from God. You may not find answers – that isn't the point – it is the questions that open you up to talking and listening to God.

Be patient toward all that is unsolved in your heart and try to love the questions themselves, like locked rooms and like books that are now written in a very foreign tongue. Do not now seek the answers, which cannot be given you because you would not be able to live them.
And the point is, to live everything. Live the questions now. Perhaps you will then gradually, without noticing it, live along some distant day into the answer.
Rainer Maria Rilke

Spiritual direction – Most retreat centers offer a time to meet with a spiritual director, usually once each day for about an hour. This may be included in the price or may be an additional charge.

Especially after spending time alone with God, talking out loud with a companion is another opportunity for awareness, finding new insight, and gaining feedback and direction.

Movement – Don't forget to move during your retreat. Walk with God in nature. Take a bike ride. I am always surprised at a sudden feeling of restlessness I experience while on retreat. I may be overcome by tiredness or more distracted. I can't focus. This signals to me that it is time to move. Or it's a perfect time to walk outside if the weather permits or down long hallways, exploring the nooks and crannies of the building.

Worship – Spending time intentionally thanking and praising God fits naturally into the retreat time. Some centers include formal worship services.

All these activities and possibilities make the retreat sound busy and full. Remember to choose what you want and need and allow time to rest. I know some retreatants who spent the majority of time sleeping as they were in such need for respite. God is good and will guide you just what you need.

Questions

1. What elements would you like/need in retreat schedule?

2. Make note of something you would want to bring along that isn't listed in this chapter. Pray for clarity if you really need to pack it.

3. What faith practices feed your spirit and draw you closer to God? Is there a new discipline to try on a retreat?

Blessing

Welcome this time away.

Enter the door of silence.

Say hello once again to your own voice so often drowned out by the world, worries, and war of life.

Knock and God will open the door and you will cross the threshold together into God's ballroom for the dance.

Drink in his hospitality.

Wrap yourself up in the warm, protecting prayers of others.

Enjoy the delightful rest.

See God play in nature and move beside you.

Embrace this gift of slowing down with God.

Enfold yourself into the present.

Greet this new experience with God.

Pause before Proceeding: The Post Retreat Re-entry

Be strong. Take courage. Don't be intimidated. Don't give them a second thought because God, your God, is striding ahead of you. He's right there with you. He won't let you down; he won't leave you.
Deuteronomy 31:6 The Message

I actually skipped and gleefully yelled "*Yippee!*" when we arrived at that Florida Welcome Center. My patient hubby just shook his head at my little girl antics.

We enjoyed their warm hospitality and left refreshed and ready for the rest of the long drive to our final destination. The rest area isn't meant to be a permanent home. We had miles to go on the busy, hectic, crazily noisy highway.

My arms were crammed with informational brochures and my heart full with anticipation of what lay ahead. I paused before getting into the car for one more look at the palm trees that symbolized my passage into this time away. I wanted to remember this moment and hold just a bit longer onto the light freeing feeling of joy.

A retreat can be the same way.

You begin the last day of the retreat sometimes with mixed feelings. Tensions arise between wanting to stay longer yet, knowing the time has come to return home.

How do you prepare for re-entry into the real world and those routines that both fuel and drain you? How can we best prepare our spirits for real life?

I find waking up on the last day, I begin my journey home before I actually leave. I start thinking of my family, my work, and wonder about the emails waiting. My to-do list nibbles at my nerves. I feel the tension slowly seeping into my cells again and want to shout *"not yet! I am still here."*

It is hard to stay mindful in the present moment when the urgent gnawing of the future chews away of your peace and quiet.

Spending time away in a safe space and in a new routine is like being an astronaut. One moment we are floating weightlessly and the next barreling and being jolted back to earth.

I stand in two worlds on that final day – one foot lingering on retreat and the other pulling me back into the world. How do I live in this tension while still cultivating the gifts I am finding while slowing down with God?

I find each retreat is special in its own way. Some have been life changing and healing for me. My imagination takes me to wondering what if time stood still and I stayed here forever.

Other times I felt I had completed what God wanted me to do and explore and it is time to go home. I leave rested and nourished. My heart and head overflow with love and new insights.

Each retreat experience presents a gift, but some retreats I have to pay more attention to find and expend more energy to dig up the pearl from the ground. I like finding a symbol for each time away to help me remember and honor that experience.

The questions for the re-entry phase are these: How do we continue being with God in everyday real life? How can we continue to experience this holy space once home in the reality of noise, commotion, and demands?

Last Day Tools – Sacred Space

On retreat we enter into a sacred space and walk on holy ground. God continues to be with us, within us, and around us no matter where we live, work, and play. The location doesn't matter, but amidst the chaos of everyday life, it is hard to hear him, to experience him, and even remember him when our focus is splattered in so many directions.

I have found before I leave a retreat to think about how God has transformed me so I can now live more connected with him. Taking the time and pondering the acronym **SPACE** helps me make the most of the last day on retreat and the re-entry into reality.

SPACE stands for Savor, Pearl, Ask, Commit, and Expectations.

S - Savor

On the last day of retreat, savor the time you have left. Don't rush. Continue to walk in an unhurried fashion. Chew your food intentionally. Pack slowly. Relish the memories.

Focus on the present time and gently postpone thoughts of home, work, and life worries. Set them aside for now.

Reread your journal.

Dance with gratitude for the time away, the lessons learned, the quiet of hearing your voice and listening to God. What a gift a retreat has been for your soul to "catch up" with your body and to be whole. I have even written a thank you note to God, thanking him for our time together.

Think about what you experienced on retreat. Maybe a new way of seeing a recent situation or a troubling relationship. Possibly you let go and surrendered a memory. Some people leave retreat feeling healed of a past experience.

On a recent retreat I spent time reviewing, processing and talking with God about a particularly rough day and all the residual negative feelings I still carried in my heart about those hurts. I gained new insights, realized how bruised my ego was and felt healed and ready to move on. The retreat provided a safe place and adequate time to hear myself clearly, see God's hand in those moments, and to gain strength from him to let go.

P – Pearl

"The kingdom of heaven is like treasure hidden in a field. When a man found it, he hid it again, and then in his joy went and sold all he had and bought that field. Again, the kingdom of heaven is like a merchant looking for fine pearls. When he found one of great value, he went away and sold everything he had and bought it."
Matthew 13: 44-45

What pearl of great value will you take home with you symbolizing this time away with God? Has an image, word, song, or verse resonated with you which describes your experience?

Take a walk and ask God for this gift. Watch for it. Review the retreat time, searching for a thread, a theme, a surprise or a joy.

I anticipate finding these pearls each time, but I don't stress over the search. Often the final gift from God doesn't appear until the final day.

I ask God for a pearl, I seek one and pay attention and celebrate with gratitude when it surfaces. If I try to force it – I may miss the real gift. I seem to know I found it when the gift arrives wrapped in love and tied with a colorful bow of wonder and surprise.

Sometimes the pearl appears in my writings. Other times my spiritual director notices it and brings it to my attention. On walks, a rose or stone appears that holds meaning for my retreat.

Watch. Pay attention. Listen.

A – Ask

What questions do you need to take home with you that arose during the retreat or still linger in your heart?

Make a list of those unanswered wonderings you recorded in your journal. Ponder in the silence what is still bubbling in your soul, seeking to be heard.

Were there any books or other ideas you want to further explore once home?

What theme is inviting you to stretch and grow?

Is there someone in our faith history you want to read about and study? What is the story of their life and their journey with God?

What is your next step? What is the waiting invitation?

What do you want to leave, let go before you return home?

What surprised you the most on retreat?

What will you tell others about your time away? What will you keep in your heart and relish just between you and God?

C- Commit

What commitment do you want to make to yourself as you return home?

You may commit to deepening the practice that refreshed you while you were away. Make a list of those faith disciplines that nourished your spirit and ponder how to best keep using them once home.

Plan ahead to make an appointment with yourself and God to revisit what you learned on retreat.

One thing I do is to write three times on my calendar to review my journal and spend some time in prayer focused on that recent experience. To be honest, I don't often make it all three times, but have learned if I set the goal, at least once happens.

On one retreat, the sacred space of the chapel drew me deeper into silence. I felt like that was the threshold place to enter in. I wanted that kind of experience at home.

I decided to create a sacred space on one side of my office. I made a small altar that enhances a time of quiet and provides some privacy.

The items I gathered for my home altar provide meaning for. I display a cross, a candle, the icon of the Trinity, the statue representing that I am always in God's hand, the drawing reminding me I am his child, a shell holding my dreams and a stone with the word "wisdom" signifying my work. I need these reminders daily so I can more easily place my hopes and work on God's altar, not in my ego's selfish grasp. I assemble my Bible, journal, favorite pen and devotional into one basket near my chair. I have no excuses for breaking the silence and stillness if everything is close by.

Seeing the altar as I enter my office helps me remember who I am serving. I once again enjoy time of silence that I experienced on retreat. I light the candle and I feel a peace enter my body as the Spirit calms my soul. I bow before my Lord and King. Sometimes I play soft music or the sounds of ocean waves, but usually silence creates the best environment for my spirit.

I discovered creating a sacred space at home helps me to experience God more deeply and settles me into a listening mode rather than a *"tell God what he ought to be doing"* approach. Hearing his voice amidst the reality of home and work grounds me and refreshes me similar to my time on retreat.

To pray is to listen, to move through my own chattering to God,
to that place where I can be silent
and listen to what God may have to say.
Madeleine L'Engle

E-Expectations

Slowly imagine your re-entry. See your family as they really are. My hubby isn't a run-to-the-door-welcome-home-honey type of guy. He will look up from the television or computer and smile and say *"glad to have you home."*

I would love to have him ask me how the retreat went, but he rarely does. I love him and accept that quirk of his personality, so know not to have that unrealistic expectation.

I also realistically acknowledge that my adult kids may have never noticed I was gone for four days. Nope, it won't happen.

> ***When you stop expecting people to be perfect, you can like them for who they are.***
> ***Donald Miller***

Don't expect things to be radically different. You are the one coming home transformed – those we left behind probably stayed the same.

The same laundry, dirty dishes and mess on the table will still be there. What I find is my perspective has changed. I am thankful for a washing machine that works and the food eaten on the dishes. And that pile of papers – sometimes I have to dig deep to find something good about them – then I smile and am thankful I have a house to come home to that holds such nuisances as unkempt, scattered papers.

Unrealistic expectations set us up for failure and negative feelings of disappointment, and hurt. Busyness sucks us back into its turmoil quite quickly. We arrived at the retreat center with an open and willing spirit. Take that same prayer into our homes and return to routine.

Use the concept of SPACE to best prepare yourself for re-entry into life. Be gentle with yourself. Kind to your spirit.

You may be coming down from a "mountaintop" experience and the valley of day to day duties isn't as appealing. The challenge for all of us is to grow from what we experience and apply its lessons to all aspects of our life.

Once Home

Give yourself space. Breath in deeply. Smile. Savor that feeling of being calmer and clearer.

Intentionally create pockets of silence throughout your day.

***We can't always withdraw to quiet hillsides to pray, but Christ will meet with us in the quiet places of our hearts.
Sheila Walsh***

Honor your family and commitments.

One aspect of the retreat is the practice of slowing down as mentioned in the last section. Create times to slow down with God in all aspects of your life.

I mentioned in the first section that vacations, including vacations with God, come in three parts. The pleasure and rewards of taking a vacation start with the anticipation of the event, embracing the present while on the trip, then reliving and enjoying the memories. This is the time to embrace the gifts from the retreat and cherish the souvenirs from your time with God.

Perseverance – keep your prayer and time with God a priority. Look at your schedule: What could you rearrange? Where could you carve out a time with God at home? If you can't find a daily time, strive for a weekly sacred appointment.

When my kids were young and I worked fulltime, the only time I could find for some quiet time with God was an occasional Sunday afternoon. I would read my Bible and write in my journal, noting how I felt God moving in my life. I wrote down my hopes and dreams and prayers. I reread my words from the retreat, grounding myself once again in that experience and its lessons.

Talk with a spiritual director or trusted friend about what you learned and how you hope to continue to walk more deeply with God. Sharing, exploring, and discussing with a trusted companion will continue to nourish your faith.

Decide when to take your next retreat. Maybe you know right now or maybe it will just be a thought like "next year." I find I need to go on retreat at least once a year and miss that practice if I skip it.

Retreat time is the flagship piece of the year that sets the standard for a rhythm of life.
Joan Chittister

Jesus spent most of his time with people, in the demands of his calling. He understands. He knows how we feel. He models for us practices to talk and be with God. We are to imitate his practice of *"going off to a quiet place"* for prayer.

Learning to live a reflecting and discerning life each day is a challenge in this noisy, stressful world. Choose wisely how you will spend your time. We can learn with time, perseverance, and God's help to live in the awareness of God, regardless of our circumstances.

Be gentle with yourself. Be flexible. Just as you did some preparing before the retreat, naming your intention during that time, you held it lightly practicing openness and willingness to be flexible. Remember to continue the prayer: "*Lord, help me to be open and willing.*"

The same is true of your re-entry into the noisy world. Be wary of your expectations. Be open to living in a new way, but know old habits resist and other people and our own ego prefer that things stay in our comfort zones.

We live in this world with a heart longing to return to be with God. God placed us here in this particular time and place to be shaped and to learn and grow in his ways. The world pulls us in many directions at a wild and break-neck speed, but God offers a different way to know him better.

Slowing down to be with God brings us closer to him, refocuses our hearts on him and helps us hear, discern, and affirm directions in our lives. Draw away from the noise and busyness.

Take a spiritual retreat with God.

Questions

1. How will you continue to find silence and solitude in your daily life?

2. Name one practice that refreshed you on retreat and ponder how you can continue that faith practice now that the retreat is over.

3. When will you go on your next retreat?

Blessing

Touch your eyes – may you continue to focus on what matters and see God in all things.

Touch your ears – Listen deeply for God's gentle voice of love.

Hold your head – Keep learning and finding God in daily life.

Feel your breath – May deep breaths slow you down, quiet your soul, and give your rest.

Look at your hands – May your hands hold books to study, pens to write, and provide service to others.

Wiggle your toes – May your feet take you on new adventures with God as he shows you how to live and love.

Touch your heart – God lives here within you and around you.

May you experience his voice reminding you that you are his beloved child.

May your journey continue…

Resources

Books

Going on Retreat - A Beginner's Guide to the Christian Retreat Experience by Margaret Silf

A Place for God – A Guide to Spiritual Retreats – Timothy Jones

A Living Room Retreat – Helen Cecilia Swift

In the Midst of Noise – An Ignatian Retreat in Everyday Life – Michael Campbell-Johnston

Time Away – a Guide for Personal Retreat – Ben Campbell Johnson and Paul H. Lang

Wilderness Time – a Guide for Spiritual Retreat – Emilie Griffin

Wrapped in Stillness: A Personal Retreat Guide – Laurie Guest

Whispers – Being God in Breath Prayers – Jean Wise

Find a Retreat Center – Where to go?

Retreat Centers with Spiritual Direction - http://www.sdiworld.org/resources/retreat-centers-with-spiritual-direction

Find the Divine - http://www.findthedivine.com

Retreat Finder - http://www.retreatfinder.com

Retreat Central - http://www.retreatcentral.com

Google retreat centers.

Call a local church/parish, or camp or state park and ask what retreat centers are nearby.

About the Author

Jean Wise has been a spiritual director since 2006 and also works as an Associate in Ministry for her church. She is a freelance journalist/writer and a speaker at retreats and gatherings.

She has written numerous devotionals, magazine articles, and newspaper features. She has several books available on Amazon including a book on prayer called ***Whispers: Being with God in Breath Prayers.***

Jean is an RN who retired from the local health department after 26 years to concentrate on a speaking and writing ministry and serving God in the second half of life. She lives in northwest Ohio with her husband as they both enjoy their empty nest. She invites you to visit her blog where she writes two times a week: http://www.healthyspirituality.org.

Made in the USA
Middletown, DE
11 January 2018

Made in the USA
Columbia, SC
20 September 2019